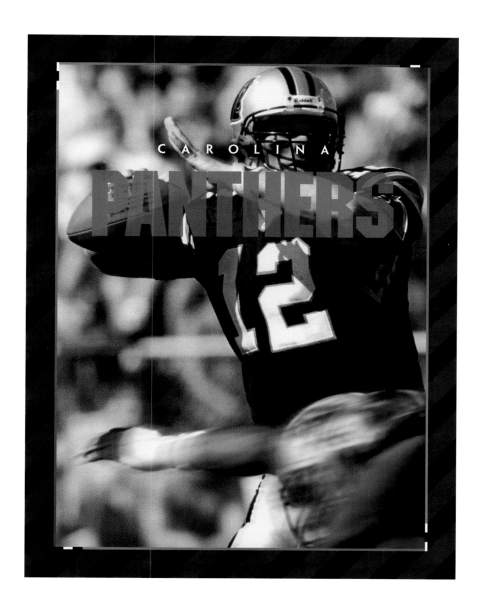

CAROLINA
PANTHERS

MICHAEL GOODMAN

CREATIVE ☙ EDUCATION

Published by Creative Education
123 South Broad Street, Mankato, Minnesota 56001
Creative Education is an imprint of The Creative Company

Designed by Rita Marshall
Cover illustration by Rob Day

Photos by: Allsport Photography, Fotosport, and SportsChrome.

Library of Congress Cataloging-in-Publication Data

Goodman, Michael E.
Carolina Panthers / by Michael Goodman.
p. cm. – (NFL Today)
Summary: Traces the history of the team from its beginnings through 1996.
ISBN 0-88682-806-6

1. Carolina Panthers (Football team)–History–Juvenile literature.
[1. Carolina Panthers (Football team) 2. Football–History]
I. Title. II Series.

GV956.C27G66 1996   96-15228
796.332'64'09756–dc20

9 8 7 6 5 4

C harlotte, North Carolina, is one of America's fastest-grow-ing cities. Lots of people come to Charlotte every day to do business, and many settle there. They are impressed by the city's blend of traditional Southern grace and modern attitude. It is the third largest banking center in the United States and a leader in manufacturing and commerce, too.

While Charlotte has experienced a major growth spurt in recent years, the city has a long and storied history. It was founded by British settlers in 1746 and named after the royal wife of King George III of England. (Because of this, people some-times refer to Charlotte as "the Queen City.") Despite their town's

The Panthers were strong believers in team effort.

With a 7-9 record, Dom Capers had the most successful first-year expansion record ever.

connection to the English rulers, Charlotte's citizens were fiercely anti-British during the American Revolution. British general Cornwallis later called the town a "hornet's nest" because of the stinging blows that local soldiers struck against his army near there. Charlotte's citizens have always been proud of Cornwallis's remark. When the city was looking for a good name for its new professional basketball team in the late 1980s, the choice was obvious: the Hornets.

Charlotte's basketball team was an immediate success and set records for attendance. The leaders of the National Football League took note of this. When the league began making plans to award two new expansion franchises, it welcomed a bid from Charlotte-area business leaders. In October 1993, the NFL awarded its 29th franchise to the Carolina Panthers.

That was only the start, however. The club was scheduled to begin play in September 1995. That meant that, in less than two years' time, a coaching staff and management team had to be put together, players had to be recruited and signed, construction had to begin on a new stadium and fans had to be won over for a new sports adventure in the Southeast. All of that was accomplished...and more.

The Panthers, who took the field at the start of the 1995 season under head coach Dom Capers were a blend of veterans and rookies, all out to establish something special together on their new club. They included veteran quarterback Frank Reich and top college draft pick Kerry Collins, the team's quarterback of the future; long-time pros like receivers Don Beebe and Mark Carrier, tight end Pete Metzelaars, safety Brett Maxie, linebacker Lamar Lathon and placekicker John Kasay; as well as youngsters like kick returner Eric Guilford, offensive linemen

Mark Carrier was a potent offensive weapon in 1995 (page 7).

Andrew Peterson and Blake Brockermeyer and defensive back Tyrone Poole.

These new football heroes are similar to the pioneers who settled the town of Charlotte 250 years ago. They are confident that they are laying the groundwork for great things to come.

1 9 9 5

Veteran wide receiver Don Beebe brought instant credibility to the Panthers passing game.

JERRY RICHARDSON SCORES BIG

The real pioneer of professional football in the Carolinas is a former pro wide receiver turned millionaire businessman named Jerry Richardson. Richardson's journey from football player to football owner took nearly 35 years. Like everything else he has accomplished in his life, the transition took hard work, determination and a little luck.

Richardson was born in a small town in North Carolina and attended Wofford College in Spartanburg, South Carolina, where he earned small college All-American honors. He often dreamed about playing professional football, and he got that chance with the Baltimore Colts for two seasons, 1959 and 1960.

Richardson was a long shot to make the Colts in 1959. "The first day in camp," Richardson recalled, "Baltimore coach Weeb Ewbank said he planned to keep just two wide receivers, and 19 were in camp. Two of them were Raymond Berry and Lenny Moore [future Pro Football Hall of Fame players], so I wasn't bursting with enthusiasm at my chances."

Nevertheless, Richardson made the team and was also named the club's top rookie that year. He even caught a touchdown pass in Baltimore's 31-16 victory over the New York Giants for the 1959 NFL championship. "That pass has become legendary—in the Richardson family," he noted with a smile.

Each Colts player received $4,864 as a winner's bonus, and Richardson decided to invest his money. He joined with a friend to buy the first Hardee's fast-food restaurant franchise, which opened in Spartanburg in October 1961. Richardson then retired from football to concentrate on business. The two partners used the profits from that first restaurant to purchase more fast-food franchises. By the mid-1970s, Richardson's company, Spartan Food Systems, was listed on the New York Stock Exchange.

Quarterback Frank Reich gave veteran leadership to the Panthers in their opening year.

But pro football continued to occupy a strong place in Richardson's heart. He began to think about owning a team that would be located in Charlotte and would represent both North and South Carolina.

"This region and its people have been so good to me and my family that there was never any question of what we wanted to do. My dream was returning something to this special area," he said.

The dream started to take shape in 1987, when the NFL announced a competition to determine which two cities would be awarded expansion franchises in the early 1990s. Richardson and his son Mark, a former football star at Clemson University and a financial expert, gathered a group of business and financial leaders in Charlotte to spearhead that city's entry into the competition. The group believed Charlotte would be an ideal candidate for an NFL franchise. The city was growing rapidly and was already among the 30 largest metropolitan areas in the United States. It also had a strong college football tradition, with powerhouses such as Clemson and the University of North Carolina nearby. The group was certain that those fans could be won over to support a new NFL club.

Rookie quarterback Kerry Collins (#12) (pages 10-11).

Following the meeting, Mark Richardson went to Kansas City to meet with architects who would draw up plans for a state-of-the-art NFL stadium to be built in the Charlotte area. Meanwhile, Jerry Richardson began drawing up other sets of plans to finance the expansion franchise and to convince the NFL that Charlotte was the right place to locate a new team. On December 15, 1987, father and son, representing a new group called Richardson Sports, officially announced Charlotte's entry into the NFL sweepstakes.

1 9 9 5

Cats collide! The Panthers battled the Jaguars in the Hall of Fame Game.

THE ROAD TO VICTORY

The Richardsons were used to winning in both football and business. And they expected to be successful in the NFL expansion competition, too. It was time to get to work to make the Carolina Panthers a reality.

The next six years were a blur of activity. The first step was to find the right man to take charge of putting the new club together. Jerry Richardson's football and business instincts told him that the best person for the job was 3,000 miles away in Seattle, Washington.

In April 1989, Richardson interviewed Mike McCormack, the man running the Seattle Seahawks. McCormack was an expert in the football business. He had been a Hall of Fame lineman for the Cleveland Browns in the 1950s, helping that team to capture back-to-back NFL titles in 1954 and 1955. Following retirement as a player, McCormack served as head coach in both Baltimore and Seattle. In 1983, he left the field for the front office when he was appointed president and general manager of the Seahawks. He quickly helped to turn a mediocre team into a success both on the field and at the box office. When he took over in Seattle, the club had 51,000 season ticket holders and had never made the playoffs. In the next six seasons, the Seahawks made the playoffs four times and not only sold out their 61,000 season tickets but had a waiting list of 29,000 more fans.

McCormack explained his ideas for putting together a management team for the Panthers, and Richardson felt that McCormack had the interest and expertise to do the job right. McCormack was hired as a consultant to Richardson Sports and later became Carolina's first team president.

Hiring McCormack was only the first step. Step two was to build enthusiasm for professional football in the Carolinas and to let the NFL see that excitement. Richardson Sports convinced the NFL to hold an exhibition game before the 1989 season at Carter-Finley Stadium in Raleigh, North Carolina. Billed as "Carolinas Kickoff '89," the game between the New York Jets and Philadelphia Eagles was an immediate sellout. Exhibition games were also held prior to the 1990 and 1991 seasons in Chapel Hill, North Carolina, and Columbia, South Carolina. Again, the games were played before packed houses, providing further proof that fans in the Carolinas were ready for a club of their own.

In the meantime, Richardson Sports began work on step three of their plan: financing and building a new stadium. By early 1990, the group had selected a site in uptown Charlotte for a pro football stadium that would hold more than 70,000 people. Unlike most NFL stadiums, this one was going to be privately financed. No tax money from either North or South Carolina or the city of Charlotte would be used to pay for it.

The Panthers logo was chosen to represent their fierce playing attitude.

Wide receiver Eric Guliford found a chance to shine in the Panthers offensive system.

"Why should someone who has no interest in football and would never go to a game have his taxes increased so a stadium could be built?" asked Mark Richardson.

Instead, Richardson Sports announced a plan involving the sale of Permanent Seat Licenses (PSLs) to finance the building. According to this plan, individuals or groups would pay up to several thousand dollars for the rights to purchase season tickets in different sections of the new stadium. There would also be luxury suites and club boxes to bring in some additional moneys.

The NFL gave its approval to this novel financing approach in 1992, and at the same time announced that the number of expansion competitors had been reduced to five: Baltimore, St. Louis, Memphis, Jacksonville and Charlotte. But the NFL leadership still wanted to see if the people in the Carolinas would "buy" the PSL idea.

July 1, 1993, was set as the first day for accepting orders for PSLs. Richardson Sports' offices in Charlotte were deluged with mail that day. By the end of the afternoon, all 8,300 club seats had been sold, all 104 luxury suites had been reserved and a total of 41,632 PSL orders had been received. By August 31, nearly 50,000 PSLs had been purchased and a total of $112.7 million was pledged for the new stadium.

Mark and Jerry Richardson headed to the NFL offices in New York to present their good news. The league was obviously impressed. Two months later, at their meeting in Chicago, the other NFL owners unanimously accepted the Carolina Panthers as the league's 29th team and the first expansion franchise since 1976, when Tampa Bay and Seattle joined the league. In late November, the Jacksonville Jaguars were also added to the NFL as its 30th franchise. Both teams were scheduled to begin play in September 1995, less than two years away.

Panthers linebacker Lamar Lathon put a stop to opposing rushers.   15

Tim McKyer had a career interceptions record of 29 before joining the Panthers.

The Panthers were assigned to the Western Division of the NFL's National Football Conference, where they would be up against the San Francisco 49ers, who had already won five Super Bowls, as well as the St. Louis Rams, Atlanta Falcons and New Orleans Saints. They would play their home games in 1995 at Clemson University's Memorial Stadium, 140 miles south of Charlotte, and then move into their brand new home the next season.

POLIAN AND CAPERS COME ON BOARD

The task for Richardson Sports now switched from winning a team for the Carolinas to creating a winning team. Team president Mike McCormack outlined his plan for the next two years: build a top-notch scouting staff, get good front office support, hire an innovative coach and construct a winning team. Then he got to work carrying out the plan.

First McCormack hired Bill Polian as the club's general manager to take care of the scouting and recruiting of players. Polian was an outstanding judge of football talent. He had earlier helped transform the Buffalo Bills from one of the worst teams in the NFL's American Football Conference to a four-time AFC champion and the only team ever to play in four consecutive Super Bowls. He was responsible for bringing stars such as Jim Kelly, Bruce Smith, Thurman Thomas and Andre Reed to Buffalo and then surrounding them with a solid supporting cast.

Despite his success in Buffalo, Polian lost his job when the Bills were unable to overcome their Super Bowl jinx and win any of their appearances in the title game. Buffalo owner Ralph Wilson felt that changing general managers might alter the team's

Quarterback Frank Reich excelled at reading defensive pass coverage.   17

luck, so he fired Polian. Mike McCormack thought that was a lucky break for the Panthers, and he jumped at the chance to bring Polian on board in Charlotte.

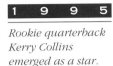

Rookie quarterback Kerry Collins emerged as a star.

"The Panthers have hired absolutely the best general manager available," said Buffalo coach Marv Levy, who had worked with Polian for many years. "They have taken the right step to come into the NFL today."

Polian's main concerns when he arrived in Charlotte were to hire a coach for the Panthers and to put together the team's first roster. The man he had in mind to lead the club on the field was Dom Capers, who had served as defensive coordinator for the Pittsburgh Steelers since 1992. What most impressed Polian about the 44-year-old Capers was his work ethic. Nobody put in more hours at his craft than Capers.

"Football is a way of life," Capers once said. "However long

it takes to get the job done, we'll do it. The most important thing is for us to be as well prepared on Sunday as we can be. We can't ever relax. If we don't take care of the little things, then we aren't going to be in a position to make a play at the end to win the game."

Capers has been taking care of details since he was a child growing up in Buffalo, Ohio, a town of 800 people with only one paved road and no stoplights. He earned spending money mowing lawns in his neighborhood. He was in big demand among the neighbors because of how carefully he carried out each job, even finishing off the edges of the lawn by hand.

Capers became a star football player both in high school and at tiny Mount Union College in Alliance, Ohio. Following college, he decided to get into coaching and served as an assistant at several top colleges. In 1984, he joined the staff of the Philadelphia Stars in the United States Football League, a short-lived professional league. Capers served under head coach Jim Mora and helped the Stars to USFL titles in 1984 and 1985. When Mora took over the reins of the NFL's New Orleans Saints in 1986, he brought Capers along as a defensive coach. Capers stayed in New Orleans for six years before heading to Pittsburgh to build one of the league's top defensive units with the Steelers.

His players in Pittsburgh were impressed with Capers as a coach and as a person. Said linebacker Levon Kirkland, "There's no barking at people, no cursing you out. He just coaches you. If he sees something, he'll tell you like a man."

After nearly 25 years as an assistant, Capers was certain that he was ready to be an NFL head coach. Bill Polian and Jerry Richardson agreed, and they offered him the job.

1 9 9 5

Punter Tommy Barnhardt helped the Panthers gain advantageous field positions.

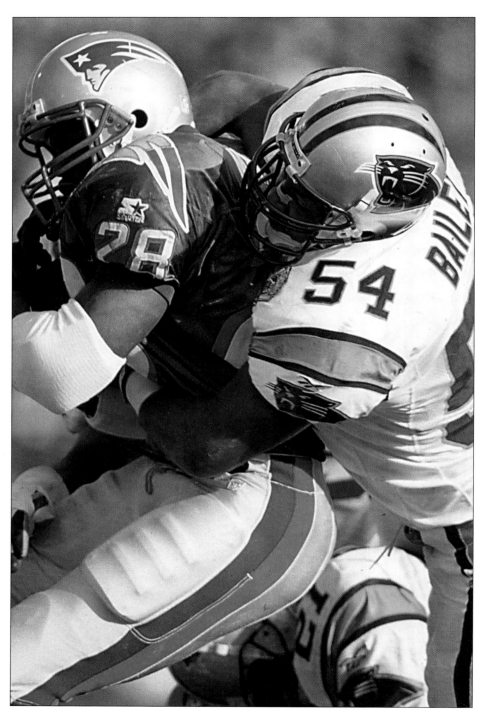

Carlton Bailey was known for his brutal tackles.

Capers joined the Panthers on January 23, 1995, only days after the Steelers were eliminated from the playoffs in the AFC Championship Game. Characteristically, he didn't waste any time. The following day he appointed offensive and defensive coordinators (Joe Pendry from the Chicago Bears and Vic Fangio from the New Orleans Saints) and met with Bill Polian and his scouting staff, who had been studying potential players for the Panthers on other NFL teams and on large and small college squads around the country.

Carolina would have three ways to select players to fill out its roster. First, there would be an expansion draft, with each of the league's 28 existing teams making available some of its unwanted young players or aging veterans for the Panthers and Jacksonville Jaguars to choose from. Second, there would be the draft of college players in the spring of 1995, with the Panthers having the first or second pick in each round. Third, there would be the opportunity to sign free agents who had decided not to re-sign with their former teams and might welcome a chance to get more playing time or more money to play in Carolina.

The expansion draft was held in February 1995, and the Panthers found several potential starters among the castoffs from the other teams. These included cornerbacks Rod Smith and Tim McKyer, receivers Mark Carrier and Eric Guilford, fullback Mark Christian and defensive tackle Greg Kragen. McKyer, who had played in two Super Bowls with the San Francisco 49ers and then anchored Pittsburgh's defensive backfield under Capers, was chosen to provide both performance and leadership in Carolina. Carrier, a former All-Pro receiver at Tampa Bay, figured to be a major cog in the Panthers' passing attack.

Running back Derrick Moore was acquired in the expansion draft from the Dallas Cowboys.

Left to right: Tim McKyer, Eric Guliford, Mike Fox, Sam Mills.

But who was going to lead that passing attack and run the Carolina offense in the team's opening season? Capers and Polian felt the team needed both an experienced signal-caller to get things started—someone who had been through the NFL "backfield wars" in the past—and an outstanding young quarterback to apprentice under the veteran and take over the team in the future. Polian immediately thought of Frank Reich, who had served as back-up to Jim Kelly during Buffalo's Super Bowl years and had started in Super Bowl XXVII in 1992. In Buffalo, Reich's specialty had been coming off the bench in pressure situations and finding a way to get the job done. There were bound to be lots of pressure situations in Carolina's opening season, since the offensive linemen protecting the quarterback would never have played together before. The 33-year-old Reich welcomed the challenge and quickly signed on with the Panthers.

Randy Baldwin, signed as a free agent, was a kick return specialist.

Polian's scouts had been almost unanimous in their choice of the best young quarterback for the Panthers to select in the upcoming college draft. The young man was big (6-foot-5, 240-pounds) and talented Kerry Collins, who had led Penn State to an undefeated season, the championship of the powerful Big Ten Conference and a Rose Bowl victory in 1994. Collins had size and arm strength and, more importantly, he had leadership skills and poise. The Panthers used the first college draft pick in their history to grab Collins.

Polian expressed great confidence in his new field general. "We feel that Kerry can lead this team for many years and that he has the tools to help us accomplish our ultimate goal: winning a Super Bowl championship. Players like that don't come along very often, so it was important for us to get him when we could."

Carolina engaged Jacksonville in the 1995 Hall of Fame Game (pages 26-27).

Sir Purr, Panthers mascot, cheered the team through its first year.

With later picks in the college draft, the Panthers took speedy cornerback Tyrone Poole from Fort Valley State, mammoth offensive tackles Blake Brockermeyer from Texas and Andrew Peterson from Washington, each over 300 pounds of muscle, and defensive end Shawn King from Northeast Louisiana University.

The two drafts had yielded some key starters for Carolina, but there were still lots of holes to fill. Polian reviewed the players who were available as free agents, particularly defensive stars and special teams performers—those who come on the field during punts, kickoffs or place-kicks. "If you look at who the great teams and champions in this league have been, you can see that great defense and special teams will win a lot of football games," Polian explained.

To bolster his team's defensive unit, Polian signed on four top linebackers—Darion Conner, Lamar Lathon, Sam Mills and Frank Stams; hard-rushing defensive end Mike Fox; and safety Brett Maxie. The key players in this group were Conner and Lathon, who would be outside linebackers in Capers' 3-4 defensive alignment.

"The two of us coming off the corner will be awesome," Conner predicted. "You look at great combinations like Pat Swilling and Rickey Jackson [with the Saints] and Carl Banks and Lawrence Taylor [with the Giants]—those guys made each other better. Lamar and I can make each other better players, too."

Conner and Lathon did just that during the Panthers' opening season in 1995. Each finished in the top 10 of the NFC in quarterback sacks, and they helped the Panthers rank as the number three defensive squad in the conference. Maxie also did his part, finishing among the leaders in the conference in pass interceptions.

Brett Maxie proudly defended the Panthers goal line.   29

Shawn King lines up to thwart an offensive play.

Tyrone Poole (#38) helps teammates level a Bear.   31

1 9 9 7

The Panthers will utilize the ferocious strength Eric Davis brings from San Francisco.

For special teams help, Polian brought in two top kickers: John Kasay, one of the most accurate field goal kickers in NFL history, and punter Tommy Barnhardt, who had played his college football at the nearby University of North Carolina. To return kicks, Polian offered a contract to free agent Randy Baldwin, the AFC's top punt returner in 1994 with Cleveland. Baldwin quickly proved that he could do much more than be a special teams performer, however. His hard work in pre-season games earned him a spot as the Panthers' number one running back.

A CLASSY DEBUT SEASON

Carolina became the most successful expansion franchise in NFL history. After starting at 0-5, a Carolina win over the New York Jets in week six at Clemson Memorial Stadium began a rush of four straight Panthers' victories. The most impressive win was a stunning 13-7 upset of the defending Super Bowl champion 49ers in San Francisco. During the streak, Kerry Collins became the starting quarterback and quickly proved he was no ordinary rookie. By season's end, the Panthers had set a new NFL first-year winning record of 7-9, and Collins had made his own mark by completing 214 passes for 2,717 yards and 14 touchdowns

The Panthers quickly sent a signal to the rest of the league that, as British General Cornwallis had discovered over 200 years earlier, teams were going to run into a "hornet's nest" when they came to Carolina to do battle. The Carolina Panthers have established that reputation as they move from expansion team to experienced competitor.